A Trial of a Trial (A Mock Trial Story)

"Objection, Your Honor…"

Catherine McGrew Jaime

Author's Note

Mock Trial, or Youth Judicial as it is sometimes called, is one of the most enjoyable, and beneficial events that my children have participated in over the years. (As of 2010, 11 out of 12 have taken part, and the younger one anxiously awaits her turn.) It is a lot of work, but they learn so much in the process!!! Not only do they get an insider's view of the judicial system, but they learn to think on their feet and to analyze facts and assumptions.

For those who are considering Law School, Mock Trial is a must! But even for those students who do not see Law School in their future, it is a very worthwhile experience. They practice public speaking, and hone their debate skills – all while having a great time.

As the coach, I enjoy Mock Trial immensely, and my goal is to have my students enjoy it as well. I encourage them to do their best, because in doing their best I believe they will get the most out of participating. Many of our students have gone on in the Competition to win awards – as top lawyers or top witnesses, etc. And many of our teams have placed very high in the state. But even those who are not "the top" or "the best" learn so much, and have fun – which are really my goals. And most come back, year after year.

This story is meant to be an example of how a "Mock Trial" can go. If you are unfamiliar with the program, it will introduce you to it. If you are familiar with it, you may be able to recognize the "good" and "bad" teams in the story. For more information on why I wrote the story, please see the Author's Credentials.

May it please the court, your honor, ladies and gentlemen of the jury...I would like to present to you a Trial[1] of a Trial.[2]

This story is based on a trial that actually occurred, with some major changes (primarily in how the judge rules on many of the objections). Names have been left out for the most part to protect the identity of the guilty!

This could be considered a humorous portrayal of what sometimes occurs or doesn't occur in our competition courtrooms – except that what really happened that one fall day wasn't funny!

Please listen carefully and come back with a verdict of guilty!

Or better yet, resolve that these are problems of the past....

---

[1] *Trial* = *"A source of vexation or annoyance"*
[2] *Trial* = *"The formal examination before a competent tribunal of the matter in issue in a civil or criminal cause in order to determine such issue."*

Judge John McGrew paced the hallway outside his courtroom. His bailiff should be signaling his entrance soon.

He heard the signal, and walked in, as the bailiff announced, "Oyez, Oyez. All rise for the honorable Judge John McGrew."

John slid into his seat, feeling once again like the king of his court. He was tired, it had been a long day; he hoped this would be an exciting trial, or he was afraid he would fall asleep while presiding.

John addressed the court, "You may all be seated", as he took in his latest group. The plaintiff lawyers sat closest to the jury – looking like they were out for blood. By all appearances, the defense lawyers were just as determined to protect their client.

After going over a few housekeeping rules (like no cell phones – how he hated cell phones going off during a trial!), and having his bailiff swear in the witnesses, he was ready to begin. He hoped the six lawyers before him were also ready.

He looked at the plaintiff table – "What says the Plaintiff?" All three plaintiff lawyers stood up in unison, and the middle lawyer at the table addressed the judge, "The Plaintiff is ready, your honor."

Good, John thought to himself, he hoped they really were ready. Addressing the other table, he enquired likewise, "What says the Defense?" One lawyer at that table stood up, and addressed him, "The Defense is ready, your honor."

John was pleased; both groups had stood when they addressed him. He didn't really care if one lawyer or all three stood at the beginning, but he was not impressed if either side dared to stay in their seats and address him; that never bode well for what he would likely think of them as the trial proceeded!

As he prepared to have the Plaintiff give their Opening Statement, John glanced again at the tables of lawyers in front of him. They all looked prepared, with their file folders and legal pads poised in front of them. The Plaintiff team had worn copies of Mauet's book on *Trial Techniques* in front of them on their table. Time would quickly tell if they really knew the topics covered in Mauet's book.

John addressed the Plaintiff lawyers: "Plaintiff, you may proceed with your Opening Statement." John had made it clear in his pre-trial conference that the attorneys would have to ask for freedom of the court. He hoped they would not stand behind their tables and try to give their Openings. The Plaintiff lawyer did not disappoint him, he requested freedom, and moved smartly to the middle, where he could see the jurors, and more importantly where they could see him! He gave a well-prepared statement, promising much. John thought to himself, *Could they deliver on all that he was promising in his Opening? That would be the real test.*

Defense followed with their Opening. It was also well-prepared, and well-delivered. At times John wondered if it had bordered on being too argumentative, but probably not.

The real trial was about to begin. Both sides had given the jury a taste of what to expect. Hopefully the jurors understood that they had not yet heard any evidence or testimony. He was always concerned that jurors would put too much stock in what was said in a well done Opening, instead of waiting for the proof throughout the trial. Either side could claim much, but they would still need to prove their points during the trial.

Plaintiff called their first witness to the stand, their expert. John reminded him that he was under oath. His lawyer asked him several background questions, establishing his expertise very efficiently. He should have been tenured easily as an expert in his field. But then the first problems began. Opposing Counsel asked to Voir Dire the Witness. John considered turning down his request, but he had been told to allow it for the competition, so he unwillingly agreed.

The Defense Lawyer came up and started grilling the Witness on very technical medical issues. There was no way this student could know these answers, the questions were so far outside the case materials. But the Witness never let on. He just kept his composure, made up answers on the spot, and sounded very much like an expert in the process.

The Defense Lawyer tried to correct the Witness, giving the correct answers to his own questions. John thought he sounded like he was reading straight from Wikipedia. The Plaintiff Lawyer was quickly on her feet. "Objection, your honor, Opposing Counsel is testifying." John agreed, brought the painful Voir Dire to a close, tenured the Witness as an expert, and let the Plaintiff Lawyer go back to her Direct.

Unfortunately, the problems had just begun. As the Plaintiff Lawyer asked the next Direct question, Opposing Counsel objected to leading. John looked up from his notes, and asked the Directing Lawyer to repeat her question for him. The question was not leading. He looked at Opposing Counsel, and sternly ruled on the objection, "Overruled".

The Plaintiff Lawyer repeated the question for her witness, and then went on to the next question. Again, an objection of leading. John was not pleased, it was going to be a long trial. There was no need to even ask for a response, it was a bogus objection. "Overruled," he replied, adding a little more emphasis to try to get the lawyer's attention. The lawyer must have caught the tone of John's voice, because he dropped the leading objections.

As the Plaintiff Lawyer was asking the witness for his opinion on a key point, Opposing Counsel objected yet again, this time to opinion. The Plaintiff Lawyer quickly replied that he was an expert, so he was allowed to give his opinion. *Good response,* thought John, as he overruled the objection.

"Then I would like to object that he is giving his opinion on the ultimate issue," countered Opposing Counsel. John inwardly groaned before responding, "This is a Civil Case, not a Criminal Case. An Expert may give their opinion in a Civil Case. Objection overruled."

Plaintiff finally finished directing their first witness; they had made their case well with their expert. The witness handled the Cross questions smoothly, making it very clear to the jury that he knew what he was talking about.

His lawyer came back on Re-Direct with a couple of well-placed questions, clearing up any possible confusion from the Cross.

Opposing Counsel tried to come back with a new topic for his Re-Cross. Apparently he hadn't liked some answers from his earlier Cross and wanted to try again. The Plaintiff Lawyer was ready for him. She sprang to her feet, "Objection, your honor, this is outside the scope of my Re-Direct." Finally, an objection that made sense! John quickly sustained the objection, and the first witness was done. *One down, five to go,* John thought gloomily to himself. This could be a long trial indeed.

Plaintiff began directing their second witness. Immediately after the background questions came Opposing Counsel's next objection, "Leading." *Not again,* John thought, *Do I have to give these lawyers a lesson in what leading is?* "Objection overruled." He hoped the firmness of his voice would get the point across. Apparently it had not. Next question, next objection, "Leading."

John had had enough. He looked at the Defense lawyers, and said very slowly, hoping the meaning of his words would not be lost on them. "If you do not have a legitimate objection to make, please make no objection at all. These questions have not been leading, and you are impeding the process of the trial by continuing to object with inappropriate objections. Do I make myself clear?" Apparently he had, because the leading objections finally came to an end, and soon this Direct was over. Cross, Re-Direct, and Re-Cross went smoothly, and two witnesses were finally done.

Plaintiff called their final witness to the stand. *Let's see what kind of objections we get this time around,* John thought to himself. Surely they've had enough of the leading objections. Plaintiff asked a question about something the witness had been told. John waited to see if Opposing Counsel would come back with an objection of Hearsay. This time they did not disappoint him.

"Objection, your honor, hearsay."

Finally, an objection that we can hear a response to, John told himself. *I can't believe it's taken this long to be able to ask this.*

He looked at the Directing Lawyer, "Is there a response?"

"Yes, your honor. This is not hearsay; it is not being offered to prove the truth of the matter asserted. In fact, what was said turned out to be false, so it cannot be hearsay."

Very good response, thought John. "Overruled." But at least this had been a legitimate objection. Direct continued.

On another question, the witness had gotten about six words into her response when Opposing Counsel objected to Narrative. *Narrative?* thought John, *please!*

"Counsel, it takes more than six words to be a Narrative response, please wait until the witness is actually narrating before you make that objection. Objection overruled." Eventually this Direct was over too.

As the Crossing Lawyer began his questions, Plaintiff finally got another chance to make an objection. Opposing Counsel started asking questions about the witness's family. Plaintiff stood up immediately, objecting, "Relevance?"

Opposing Counsel tried to come up with a response, but John was not convinced of the relevance of that topic. "Sustained."

Counsel moved on to another topic, Plaintiff again argued Relevance. This time the Defense lawyer had a better response, and John overruled the objection. *Finally, some good objections and responses,* John thought to himself, *I've waited long enough.*

Cross finally ended. The Cross had been short and fairly ineffective, so the Plaintiff lawyer passed on the opportunity for a Re-Direct. John looked at the witness, "Since there is no Re-Direct, there will be no Re-Cross. Witness may step down."

Finally, they were at the half-way point of the trial. John looked at the Plaintiff lawyers, "Does the Plaintiff have any other witnesses to call?"

Standing, one of their lawyers responded: "No your honor, the Plaintiff rests."

Good, John thought, *Let's see what Defense has to offer us.*

"Defense, you may call your first witness."

Defense called their witness to the stand. The Direct was long and tedious. It appeared that they were going to cover every possible topic from the Witness's statement.

Very interesting, John pondered the line of questioning. *What is the point of these questions?* He asked himself.

Direct was finally over and the Crossing Lawyer stood and asked his first question. Defense came back to objecting quickly, "Asked and answered." John couldn't believe his ears. "Asked and answered?" It was the first question of his Cross; he couldn't have already asked it! He looked at the Defense lawyer in disbelief.

Before John could say anything, the Defense Lawyer continued, "I asked that question on my Direct. It's been asked and answered."

The lengthy Direct was coming into a very upsetting focus for John. Once again, he didn't need to wait for a response. "Objection overruled. This question was asked on Direct, not on Cross, therefore 'asked and answered' does not apply."

What do they teach these lawyers? John thought to himself.

Cross finally continued. John was afraid to think about what objections might lay ahead. Sure enough, after a couple more Cross questions, the Defense lawyer stood and made yet another objection: "Leading, your honor."

John was stunned. *Leading? Yes, it was a leading question this time – counsel had that part correct – but this was Cross, of course counsel was leading!*

There was no need for a response yet again. "Overruled, this is Cross, leading is allowed." (*In fact, it's encouraged*, John thought to himself!)

There is certainly no shortage of objections during this trial, John thought. Falling asleep was not going to be a problem. Keeping calm, on the other hand, was proving quite difficult.

This Cross eventually ended, as did the Re-Direct and Re-Cross. One more witness done!

The second Defense witness took the stand. John reminded her that she was under oath. This was the Defense's expert witness. After establishing her credentials, the Directing Lawyer began asking her questions that involved her expertise.

The Plaintiff Lawyer immediately stood up: "Objection, your honor, opinion of a lay witness."

Very good, thought John. *They've been paying attention.* "Is there a response?"

Opposing Counsel shot back, "This not a lay witness, this is our expert."

John smiled to himself. He knew what the Plaintiff's response was going to be, even as he asked: "Response?"

Plaintiff Counsel argued "This witness has not been tenured as an expert; therefore she is only a lay witness at this time, your honor."

"Objection sustained." *Now let's see if the Defense Lawyer knows what to do next*, John thought.

Fortunately, the Defense Lawyer had figured out his mistake. "Your honor, we would like to tenure this witness as an expert in psychology."

John looked back at the Plaintiff Lawyer, "Is there any objection?"

"Yes, you honor, we believe that this is too broad for his credentials. We would ask that it be narrowed down."

Back to the Defense: "Response?"

"Your honor, we will limit his expertise to clinical psychology."

"Objection?"

"No, your honor, no objection."

"So entered."

Defense proceeded with their questions, drawing no further objections from the Plaintiff.

Cross. Re-Direct. Re-Cross. The fifth witness finished quickly.

"Defense, you may call your third witness."

The Defense Lawyer got through the introductory questions and then asked to approach her witness with an exhibit.

"For what purpose?"

"Identification purposes"

"Yes, you may."

Immediately after having had her witness identify the exhibit, Counsel started asking him to read from the document. As John anticipated, Opposing Counsel was on his feet immediately: "Objection, your honor, this document has not been entered into evidence."

No need to ask for a response on this objection: "Objection sustained." Feeling like Defense was in need of some assistance, John turned to the Defense Lawyer: "Counselor, you must enter an exhibit into evidence before you can have a witness testify from it."

The Defense Lawyer fumbled through the mechanics of entering the exhibit and then continued on with her questions.

John could finally see an end in sight to this painful trial. *When this Direct ends, we will be almost done with witness' testimonies*, he thought excitedly.

John was brought out of his momentary lapse of attention by an objection from the Plaintiff Lawyer.

"Objection, your honor, unfair extrapolation. This is outside the scope of his statement and materially alters the case."

Uh oh, he thought to himself. *What did I miss?*

Looking at the Defense Lawyer, John slowly asked, "What was the question?"

Plaintiff interrupted, "Your honor, I was objecting to the answer being given, not the question."

"One step at a time," John calmly responded. "The question, please."

After the Defense Lawyer repeated the question, John inquired of the witness: "And what was the answer you were giving before the objection?"

The witness repeated it and John looked back at the Plaintiff Lawyer, pondering the question and answer he had just heard. "What specifically were you objecting to?"

"Your honor, the witness's statement does not go into those types of details, and adding them now materially alters this case."

John agreed, it was unfair extrapolation. "Objection sustained." John thought to himself, *Opposing counsel could have dealt with this on Cross, but in this case, it was probably best to just get it out of the way immediately.*

The Directing Lawyer reworded her question slightly and the Witness came back with a similar answer.

Opposing Counsel was on his feet again: "Objection, your honor, this answer has already been ruled inadmissible."

"Objection sustained. Counsel, please move on to a different line of questioning."

Direct finally ended. The Plaintiff Lawyer did a short but effective Cross of the witness. Defense came back with a short Re-Direct. This time the Witness started giving details that were contrary to her statement. John glanced at Opposing Counsel to see if he had caught it. He had, but he did not object. He waited patiently instead. John knew what was about to happen, even if the Witness and the Defense Lawyer did not. Sure enough, when the Plaintiff Lawyer started his Re-cross, he was ready.

"Your honor, may I approach the Witness with her sworn statement." "Yes, you may."

He walked smartly over to the witness, showing the statement to Opposing Counsel on his way there. "This is a copy of your statement, correct? And this is your signature, correct? Please read along silently, as I read aloud…Did I read that correctly? You were under oath when you gave this statement? And you are under oath today? Thank you. Your honor, I have no further questions for this witness."

John looked happily at the witness, "You may sit down."

Looking at their table, he enquired: "Does the Defense have any other witnesses to call?

Standing, one of their lawyers responded: "No your honor, the Defense rests."

Closing Arguments at last! Ten more minutes, give or take, and this trial would be over! "Is the Plaintiff ready to proceed with their Closing Arguments?"

"Yes, your honor. May I request freedom of the court?"

The Plaintiff Lawyer walked smartly into the middle of the area, looking confidently at the jury, and positioning herself where she could also see the bailiff with her time.

She delivered a strong Closing, referring occasionally to her notes. As she ended, she looked back at the judge, "Your honor, I would like to reserve the remainder of my time for a rebuttal."

"That is your right."

"Is the Defense ready to give their Closing Argument?"

The Defense Lawyer also requested freedom of the court, and moved closer to the jury, too close for comfort, John noted to himself. The jury was certainly not going to fall asleep during this Closing.

Defense ended and Plaintiff came back, quickly rebutting several of Defense's key points in the final minute of her Closing, and asking the jury to come back with a verdict of guilty.

John read the jury charges, dismissed the Jury to deliberate, and called a ten minute recess. He rubbed his temples. He fully expected the jury to convict. But either way, the score sheets would show the true outcome of this trial. The Plaintiff had just outgunned the Defense at almost every turn.

As he waited, John muttered to himself the words of a song he hadn't thought about in decades: *When will they ever learn? When will they ever learn?*

Author's Credentials

I am not a lawyer, I am a teacher. I have been the primary coach of 27 homeschool Mock Trial teams over the past 13 years. Eight of those years we took 1st place at the Alabama State Competition. Ten of those years we had students chosen for the Alabama Mock Trial team competing in the National Mock Trial Competition. And in 2008, our homeschool team placed a very respectable 8 out of 18 at the American Mock Trial Invitational in Charlotte, N.C.

At this point, it would be fair to say I have a fairly good idea of what Mock Trial should look like. I have seen many good teams in our competitions, and I have seen many weak teams. Weak teams can become better – if they choose to work hard, and if they have some assistance from a coach who cares.

*But in 13 years of doing this, what has aggravated me the most are the teams who cheat. Most of this story comes from a trial we competed in where the other team acted almost identically to the Defense team here – but the difference was they didn't have John McGrew as a judge. They had a judge who let them cheat and get away with it. They managed to shut down a Plaintiff team made up of new students – students who were prepared for a lot – but not for these types of bogus objections. I wrote this story almost immediately after that trial – as my version of what **should** have happened!*

After 13 years, I don't see the benefit of that type of behavior. I want students to learn to do this right – and to enjoy themselves in the process. Maybe this will be one step in the right direction.